how to BUILD *a* MUSEUM

by Tonya Bolden

Smithsonian's National Museum of
African American History and Culture

Viking

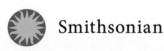

Smithsonian

History, as nearly no one seems to know, is not merely something to be read. And it does not refer merely, or even principally, to the past. On the contrary, the great force of history comes from the fact that we carry it within us, are unconsciously controlled by it in many ways, and history is literally present in all that we do. It could scarcely be otherwise, since it is to history that we owe our frames of reference, our identities, and our aspirations.

—James Baldwin, "The White Man's Guilt," 1965

Walk with the sun,
Dance at high noon;
And dream when night falls black;
But when the stars
Vie with the moon,
Then call the lost dream back.

—Lewis Alexander, "Dream Song," 1926

CONTENTS

PREFACE

A museum is a treasure trove of things. Things lost then found. Things perennially prized. Objects once deemed worthless.

Whatever a museum collects—paintings, pottery, or playthings—its aim is the same: to safeguard remnants of history and culture that inspire, enlighten, and kindle the curiosity of the children and adults who come through its doors, generation after generation.

Smithsonian's National Museum of African American History and Culture is a treasure trove of paintings, photographs, posters, playbills, pottery, documents, dolls, diaries, books, balls, bells, benches, medals, medallions, and more: objects that deepen our understanding of the black experience in America and so strengthen our grasp of American history.

This is the story of how that magnificent and monumental museum got built.

A digital image from the architect's plans for Smithsonian's National Museum of African American History and Culture (NMAAHC) in Washington, DC.

DREAM

"The meeting of the Colored Citizens' Committee for the entertainment of Old Veterans and Delegates to the G.A.R. Encampment . . . was very well attended last Saturday evening."

—*The Washington Bee*, June 19, 1915

Smithsonian's National Museum of African American History and Culture was a long time coming. It was a hundred-year hope, a hundred-year dream rooted in the desire for a tribute in the United States' capital to black patriots.

The dream began to take shape in September 1915 during a big reunion: the Grand Army of the Republic's Forty-ninth National Encampment. The GAR was an organization of veterans who had served in the Union's armed forces during the Civil War (1861–1865). Fifty years after the war ended, thousands of former servicemen from more than forty states poured into the nation's capital. They came with war wounds and disabilities, with medals and memorabilia. They came with memories of battles lost and won, of fallen comrades, of heroism unsung. Their average age was seventy-three. Despite old age and infirmities, more than twenty thousand veterans proudly marched in the big parade up Pennsylvania Avenue.

A contingent of those GAR members were African American, representing the roughly 200,000 black boys and men who had fought for

A view of the National Mall from the Smithsonian Castle, circa 1915.

September 29, 1915: The Grand Army of the Republic's parade up Pennsylvania Avenue, America's Main Street.

Far right: A photograph (circa 1864–1865) and the military I.D. tag of Sergeant Qualls Tibbs (1836–1922), a Virginia-born member of the United States Colored Troops, 27th Regiment, Company E.

Right: Souvenir badge belonging to Alexander Hill, 54th Massachusetts Infantry (1864–1865).

the Union on land and sea. During the encampment, black Washingtonians saw to it that these Civil War survivors were properly housed, fed, and feted. Civic leader and government worker Ferdinand D. Lee headed up the committee in charge of this hospitality.

Before the GAR Encampment ended on October 2, Ferdinand D. Lee and company made up their minds to take their pride in sable soldiers and sailors a step further. They rallied around an idea already in the air, and within months of the GAR reunion, Ferdinand D. Lee was at the helm of a new organization: the National Memorial Association for the Erection of a Monument at the National Capital in Honor of the Negro Soldiers and Sailors Who Fought in the Wars of Our Country. The group became known for short as the National Memorial Association (NMA).

When the NMA got going in February 1916, Washington, DC, was not the marvel of memorials, monuments, and museums that it is today. The colossal Christopher Columbus Memorial Fountain fronting Union Station was only a few years old, and the elegant

Dupont Circle fountain hadn't been erected. The capital did not have half the outdoor sculptures that it boasts today.

The National Mall, which had once been bordered by homes, shops, vendors' carts, and holding pens for enslaved people bound for the Deep South, had only a handful of splendors. They included the Smithsonian's red sandstone "Castle" building and its Arts and Industries Building, and the Washington Monument.

Four years later, in 1920, when the Lincoln Memorial was still under construction, legislation to create a commission on a memorial to black servicemen was pending in Congress, which had no African American members. There was little support for this legislation, and the bill died. Despite the setback, the National Memorial Association continued to hold rallies to raise money for a memorial. They kept lobbying politicians to support the dream. And in black communities, interest in the idea surged.

In the early 1900s, black pride was on the rise. Afro–Puerto Rican Arturo Schomburg, a bibliophile and self-taught historian, urged blacks to dig up and dig into their heritage. Jamaican-born journalist and entrepreneur Marcus Garvey launched the Universal Negro Improvement Association. Scholar-activist Dr. W. E. B. Du Bois, who helped found the National Association for the Advancement of Colored People (NAACP), was editor-in-chief of this Civil Rights organization's magazine, *The Crisis*. Month after month, *The Crisis* reported on the challenges blacks faced in the age of government-sanctioned segregation, along with black strivings and achievements despite these challenges. Another NAACP founder and an NMA member, Mary Church Terrell, crusaded for racial justice and women's rights in lectures and articles, and as a member of various organizations.

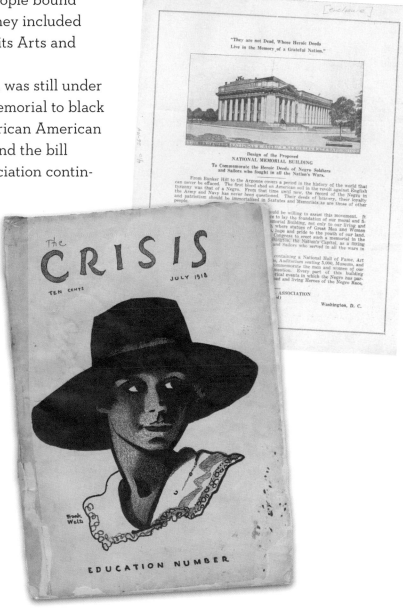

The NMA's vision of the dream, in a pamphlet circa 1926.

The July 1918 issue of W. E. B. Du Bois's The Crisis *magazine. The focus: education.*

What's more, in cities around the nation, painters, photographers, writers, singers, dancers, and intellectuals of African descent were finding and establishing more outlets for their talent. This was all part and parcel of the New Negro Movement, a push for positive representation and greater participation in politics and other areas of American life.

In this climate, the National Memorial Association began to dream bigger. By the late 1920s, it was campaigning for a first-rate museum devoted to black contributions to America's military, arts and sciences, literature, and industry—the whole universe of human endeavor.

Perseverance paid off. The NMA steadily gained more support in Congress. By March 1929, despite virulent opposition, especially from white Southern senators and representatives, a Congressional bill passed that created a committee to map out the what, where, and how of a national museum devoted to the contributions of African Americans. On his last day in office, President Calvin Coolidge signed the bill into law.

This law, however, came with a bitter pill. It appropriated up to $50,000 in public funds for the museum, but this money would not be released until the NMA raised $500,000. A hefty sum of money even now, this was a huge amount of money in 1929, when a quart of milk cost fourteen cents. What's more, disaster soon struck.

In October 1929, the stock market crashed. In its wake came the Great Depression. Millions of Americans lost jobs, homes, and all their savings. How could the NMA hope to raise a half million dollars now?

Despite economic hard times, despite entrenched and sometimes bloody racism, the bruised dream lived on, even though the NMA's driving force,

THE NATIONAL AFRICAN AMERICAN MUSEUM

Is coming...

A mid-twentieth-century pin
promoting the museum.

Ferdinand D. Lee, died in the spring of 1933. A few months later, in a reorganization scheme, President Franklin Delano Roosevelt abolished several commissions, including the one on the museum. Its work was transferred to the Department of the Interior; the museum wound up on hold.

Still, the dream lived on.

It lived on while other projects, such as the Jefferson Memorial in West Potomac Park (1938) and the National Gallery of Art (1941), became realities. The dream lived on through World War II (1939-1945), and then through momentous postwar change on the homefront arising from the Civil Rights, Black Power, women's rights, and antiwar movements.

By the late 1980s, the National Mall was home to even more museums, including Smithsonian's National Air and Space Museum. West Potomac Park had three more memorials: the Vietnam Veterans Memorial Wall, the Three Servicemen Statue, and the Memorial to the 56 Signers of the Declaration of Independence. But still the country's capital had no national museum focused on the history and culture of America's people of African descent.

Such a museum's champions now included black United States Army veteran Tommy L. Mack, owner of Tourmobile, a DC sightseeing service. In 1985 Mack launched the National Council for Education and Economic Development to urge politicians and other people to press harder for the dream.

There was also Representative John Lewis of Georgia. In 1988 this veteran of the Civil Rights movement introduced a bill for a national museum

On August 28, 1963, the March on Washington for Jobs and Freedom filled the National Mall.

Left: Civil Rights activist and member of Congress John Lewis.

The Time Has Come
Report to the President and to the Congress

National Museum of African American History and Culture
PLAN FOR ACTION PRESIDENTIAL COMMISSION

April 2, 2003

Cover of the landmark report
The Time Has Come.

devoted to black history and culture that would join the Smithsonian Institution's family of museums. It died without a hearing. But Lewis would not give up. Year after year he sponsored a bill for the dream. Another black representative, George "Mickey" Leland of Texas, and Paul Simon, a white senator from Illinois, were among Lewis's colleagues in Congress who stepped up with support.

The campaign continued through the 1990s when West Potomac Park became home to the Vietnam Women's Memorial, the Korean War Veterans Memorial, and the Franklin Delano Roosevelt Memorial. Added to the Mall: the U.S. Holocaust Memorial Museum in 1993, the same year Congress authorized a National World War II Memorial. Six years later, the National Museum of the American Indian in Washington, DC, had its groundbreaking. Then . . .

As 2001 wound down, Representatives John Lewis and J. C. Watts Jr. (Oklahoma), and two white senators, Max Cleland (Georgia) and Sam Brownback (Kansas), sponsored yet another bill to create a new commission to draft an action plan for the museum. By December 18, their bill had cleared Congress. A few days after Christmas, President George W. Bush signed it into law.

In April 2003 this new commission sent the president and Congress a report and action plan for Smithsonian's National Museum of African American History and Culture.

It was called *The Time Has Come.*

A National Museum of African American History and Culture would be dedicated to the collection, preservation, research, and exhibition of African American historical and cultural material reflecting the breadth and depth of the experiences of individuals of African descent living in the United States.

—From Public Law 108-184, which established NMAAHC

Seven months later, a bill creating the long-sought, long-fought-for museum passed in the House of Representatives, 409 to 9, and then passed in the Senate by unanimous consent. On December 16, 2003, President George W. Bush signed that bill into law.

Finally, the dream had wings!

But where would this new museum be located? Next door to the Smithsonian Institution Castle? In Smithsonian's Arts and Industries building, which was in need of renovation? Or should it get a brand-new building in Benjamin Banneker Overlook Park at the tip of L'Enfant Plaza? The debate lasted more than two years. Finally, on January 30, 2006, NMAAHC's founding director, Lonnie G. Bunch III, made a big announcement: Smithsonian's National Museum of African American History and Culture would be built on the last available acres on the National Mall, America's Front Yard.

HAVE *a* VISION

"He is charged with a task so huge it is nearly paralyzing. Bunch must build a museum from scratch—but not just any museum. He must build the last museum slated to be constructed on the Mall."

—*The Washington Post,* February 17, 2012

It takes a lot of people to build a major museum. Curators, who are specialists in a particular field or content area, are needed to help develop the museum's collection and decide what the museum should exhibit. They research and acquire objects for the museum, then brainstorm on how to display those objects. As new artifacts come in, technicians examine them and make sure they are properly stored. If there's a problem with an object, it goes on to a conservator for preservation work. And how would a museum keep track of all its holdings without specialists who catalogue and digitize every single item? Museums also need education specialists to create captivating programs, and docents (guides) to show visitors around the museum and speak about its collections.

Of course, no museum can function without men and women who are often unheralded, such as maintenance workers, security experts, accountants, administrative assistants, executive assistants, fundraising and public relations mavens, and IT specialists.

But before a museum can have a team, it needs a leader.

The National Mall with the NMAAHC building site circled.

Lonnie G. Bunch III, a native of New Jersey, was happy with his job as president of the Chicago Historical Society when he was tapped to be the founding director of Smithsonian's National Museum of African American History and Culture.

The museum didn't have a site yet.

The physical building was a long way away from being on any architectural drawing board.

Millions of dollars had yet to be raised for a building, collections, staff, and everything else a museum needs.

If Bunch said yes, all he'd have to work with was, well, the dream. But he quickly realized that he was looking at an opportunity of a lifetime—especially for someone like him who'd been crazy about history since he was a kid.

That passion for the past was kindled in his grandparents' home. Lonnie and Leanna Bunch, his father's parents, lived in Belleville, New Jersey, a few miles north of Newark, where Doc Bunch was one of that city's first licensed black dentists.

Young Lonnie was fascinated with his grandparents' basement. "The unfinished and unadorned basement was a mysterious, fertile place that stimulated my imagination." This wonderland was full of "dusty and worn remnants" of his grandparents' past, from old dental equipment to trunks stuffed with clothes and papers. And books. There were lots of books in that basement.

Lonnie was about four years old when Doc Bunch read to him from one of those old books. It had pictures from way back in the 1800s. One photograph in particular was spellbinding. "Unidentified school children." That's all the caption said.

"I wanted to know who those kids were," Bunch wrote years later. "What kind of lives did they live?" He was becoming curious about the Mondays and Sundays of everyday people who passed through

Return from the Fields *(1894) by Rudolf Eickemeyer. This photograph, taken in Mount Meigs, Alabama, is one of Bunch's beloved pieces of history. Though the woman's dress is tattered and her hands are swollen, "she's striving forward," Bunch told a reporter in 2006. "Whenever I'm ready to quit, I look at that picture and say, if she did it, so can I. That's what history does to me. History is really the greatest inspiration that we can have."*

NMAAHC founding director Lonnie Bunch once said that building a museum and its collection simultaneously was like being on "a cruise in uncharted waters at the same time that you are building the ship."

Left: Bunch (left) with Brian Flegel, vice president of Clark Construction; below: Bunch adds his signature to an iron beam that will be used in the building.

history, along with those of well-known history-makers.

Years later, Bunch majored in history in college and graduate school, then spent most of his adult life making magic at different museums. Then in March 2005 came that chance of a lifetime—and Bunch said yes.

Every director needs a deputy director. Like Bunch, this second-in-command would wear many hats, from that of fundraiser to program and exhibition developer to supervisor of the building's design and construction. For this post, Bunch recruited a visual and performance artist and veteran museum professional, Kinshasha Holman Conwill, an arts, museum, and management consultant at the time. As a child growing up in Atlanta, Georgia, Conwill had a front-row seat to many events in the Civil Rights movement. Her father was a professor of English at Clark College (now part of Clark Atlanta University) and editor-in-chief of *The Atlanta Inquirer*, a progressive protest weekly that covered the Atlanta Student Movement as no other newspaper did. From an early age, Conwill was aware and well informed.

Bunch's (right) first museum job was at the Smithsonian's National Air and Space Museum. He later served as the curator of history and program manager at the California African American Museum, and as a supervising curator, assistant director of curatorial affairs, and associate director of curatorial affairs at the Smithsonian's National Museum of American History. Before joining NMAAHC, Conwill (left) held several key positions on arts boards and in museum organizations, including senior policy advisor for the American Association of Museums and director of the Studio Museum in Harlem.

While Bunch and Conwill were building their team, they were also working on how to tell the story of blacks in America with vitality and texture, "a story all Americans were shaped by and need to know," as Bunch often said.

In a talk at Stanford University in May 2011, Bunch spoke at length about the vision for NMAAHC. It was to be a "place to help us to remember. A place to help us find meaning in the African American experience. It's a place to help us remember, oh, the names we know maybe in new ways—to think differently about Martin Luther King Jr. or Sojourner Truth or Harriet Tubman or Rosa Parks."

Would the museum feature only people already in the history books? No way. It would also remember, as Bunch put it, "the people we don't know": a nameless enslaved woman who held on to her humanity and her humor; a family who left the Deep South in the early 1900s and made its way to Chicago or another big northern city seeking better jobs, better housing, and new opportunities; a young white Northerner who went south in the early 1960s to help blacks register to vote and in so doing put his life on the line. Unsung heroes, strivers, and agents of change are legion.

Though the museum would inevitably move visitors to tears, it would not be all sorrow song. It would also be, Bunch pointed out, a place that captured "the joy of the African American community," a place where people tap their toes "to Duke Ellington or Aretha Franklin or Sam Cooke or somebody from the hip-hop generation." Above all, the museum Bunch and his team were building would drive home the point

that black history is *everybody's* history. NMAAHC would offer the world American history through the African American lens.

NMAAHC's Four Pillars

• Creating an opportunity for those who care about African American history and culture to explore and revel in this history

• Using African American history and culture as a lens through which to see what it means to be an American

• Telling the African American story in an international context

• Serving as a place of collaboration—supporting and encouraging the work of other museums and educational institutions

But what kinds of things would show the story NMAAHC wanted to tell? And where would the stuff come from? Almost from the very beginning, Director Bunch, Deputy Director Conwill, and other members of team NMAAHC were on the case—brainstorming, sleuthing, searching high and low for all kinds of things, in small towns and big cities throughout the States and around the world.

Left to right: Two enslaved women, Lucinda and Frances Hughes, doing laundry surrounded by their children, on Felix Richards's Valusia Plantation, near Alexandria, Virginia (1861–1862); young students at Fisk University in Nashville, Tennessee (undated); a carte de visite (photographic card) of a couple (1860s); a locket showing Civil Rights activists Harriette V. (top) and Harry T. Moore (bottom) of Mims, Florida. On Christmas Day 1951 the couple's home was bombed by the Ku Klux Klan (KKK). He died on the way to the hospital, she about a week later.

GO TREASURE HUNTING

"While the museum will talk about the achievements of famous African-Americans, from Frederick Douglass and the Rev. Dr. Martin Luther King Jr. to Duke Ellington and Ethel Waters, its curators are also looking for objects that will reflect the experiences of ordinary people."

—*The New York Times*, January 22, 2011

Museums build their collections all sorts of ways. They invite individuals and institutions to donate items. They pay for artifacts. They even snap up things that might otherwise end up in the trash. Smithsonian's National Museum of African American History and Culture did all this and more.

The museum was not shy about encouraging people to donate items—they asked outright! In Spring 2013, NMAAHC made a public appeal on its website:

PLEASE HELP US BY DONATING YOUR OBJECTS

We need your help!

NMAAHC is the first Smithsonian museum
to build its own collection from scratch.

We collect artifacts, historical documents, photographs, audio recordings, moving images, books, and visual arts. The museum preserves these historical materials to share with the public and future generations through exhibitions and research.

Loading in one of the two biggest objects installed in NMAAHC.

People responded in droves. Author, bibliophile, and historian Dr. Charles L. Blockson of Philadelphia, Pennsylvania, was among the many people who helped build the museum's collections. An expert on the Underground Railroad whose family tree includes people Harriet Tubman helped escape slavery in Delaware and Maryland's Eastern Shore, he donated thirty-nine artifacts from Tubman's life. A hymnal, a knife and fork, a shawl, and lace handkerchiefs were among the items Blockson officially handed over to NMAAHC in a special ceremony on March 10, 2010, the ninety-seventh anniversary of the death of the woman called "Moses."

Descendents of the white abolitionist William Lloyd Garrison donated several family heirlooms to the museum. These objects include a photograph of their noted ancestor; pictures of the Fifty-fourth Massachusetts Volunteer Infantry Regiment, one of the first official black units in the Union Army; and a gold pocket watch. A British abolitionist had given Garrison the watch in 1851 in honor of the twentieth anniversary of Garrison's antislavery newspaper, *The Liberator*.

NMAAHC also received the ensemble that opera singer Marian Anderson wore during her famous public concert in Washington, DC.

Above: A hymnal (1876) belonging to Harriet Tubman (circa 1822–1913). Tubman sometimes signaled slaves by singing hymns. She received this shawl (circa 1897) as a gift from England's Queen Victoria.

Top right: Massachusetts-born William Lloyd Garrison (1805–1879), circa 1860.

Right: Marian Anderson (1897–1993) at the Lincoln Memorial, singing for a crowd of 75,000 people; the ensemble she wore.

After the Daughters of the American Revolution, an organization supposed to promote patriotism, refused to let Anderson hold a concert in their Constitution Hall because she was black, First Lady Eleanor Roosevelt resigned from the organization and then helped arrange for Anderson to stage a concert on the steps of the Lincoln Memorial. "My Country, 'Tis of Thee" was among the songs the contralto sang on that Easter Sunday, April 9, 1939. Seventy-five years later Ginette DePriest gave NMAAHC the orange-and-black-velvet outfit Anderson had worn on the historic day. DePriest was the widow of Anderson's nephew James DePriest, a celebrated musical conductor.

Anderson's outfit was not the only wardrobe donation. NMAAHC received seven hundred garments and three hundred accessories, as well as sixty boxes of related printed matter, from DC resident Joyce Bailey.

This African American woman was not a hopeless shopaholic but the daughter of Lois K. Alexander-Lane (1916–2007), founder of the Black Fashion Museum, which opened in Harlem, New York, in 1979 and moved to Washington, DC, in the 1990s. Over the years, Alexander-Lane had collected a range of apparel, from the clothing everyday people wore to costly creations by black designers such as Ann Lowe. Alexander-Lane also collected costumes black performers wore on stage and screen.

From NMAAHC's Black Fashion Museum Collection. Top left: A dress that seamstress Rosa Parks (1913–2005) was working on before her arrest on December 1, 1955, in Montgomery, Alabama, for refusing to surrender her seat on a bus to a white person; bottom left: A skirt worn by Lucy Lee Shirley (1855–1929) as a child. She may have been born into slavery in Virginia.; bottom right: A 1966–1967 gown designed by Ann Lowe (1898–1981).

Tuskegee Airmen trained in this open cockpit biplane at Moton Air Field in Tuskegee, Alabama, during World War II. The Boeing-Stearman PT-13D Kaydet (circa 1944) was flown cross-country to NMAAHC in Summer 2011. Along the way, it passed over a gathering of surviving Tuskegee Airmen who had served their nation more than sixty years earlier. An interior part of the historic plane has been signed by more than forty of the veteran airmen.

A "Save Our African American Treasures" participant and a museum specialist.

NMAAHC got a rare find from two plane enthusiasts, Air Force captain Matthew Quy and his wife, Tina, a white couple in Sacramento, California. The Quys bought a plane, which was a wreck, at an auction in 2005, with plans to restore it. They named it the Spirit of Tuskegee after they had its serial number traced and learned that it was used during World War II to train Tuskegee Airmen, the first black pilots in the United States armed forces—men who served with distinction. NMAAHC has Dik Daso, a former military aircraft curator at the Smithsonian's Air and Space Museum, to thank for bringing this vintage plane to its attention.

NMAAHC also built its collections while being of service to the general public with its program "Save Our African American Treasures: A National Collections Initiative of Discovery and Preservation." Through the Treasures program, the museum invited people to bring up to three family heirlooms to a public library or other institution where NMAAHC conservation specialists and historians were on hand to advise them on how best to preserve, say, a one-hundred-year-old quilt, diary, or photograph.

The first daylong Treasures program was held at Chicago's Harold Washington Library Center on January 19, 2008. Among the scores of people who turned out for the event was a woman with a World War II Marine Corps uniform. It had belonged to her father, one of the first fifty black leathernecks in the modern era. Another woman brought in a white Pullman porter's cap and a badge from a 1910s convention hosted by the beauty-care company built by Madam C. J. Walker, who went from rags to riches and became one of the first black female millionaires.

Charleston, South Carolina, was another stop on NMAAHC's Treasures tour. There a woman brought in a sack that had been in her family for five generations. Sometime in the 1850s, an enslaved woman named Rose had sewn the sack in a hurry and filled it with a few pieces of clothing and a handful of pecans. This was a parting gift to her nine-year-old daughter, Ashley, who had been sold and would soon be taken away. Ashley's granddaughter, Ruth Middleton, embroidered this story on the sack in 1921, including that, as mother told daughter at the time, the sack also included all her love.

Top left: A Pullman porter was a servant aboard a special type of train car: one of George Porter's luxurious sleeping cars (something like a little apartment). From the late nineteenth through the mid-twentieth century, thousands of black men worked as Pullman porters.

Bottom left: A sack inscribed with family history brought to the Treasures public program held at Burke High School, Charleston, South Carolina, in Spring 2009.

Below: Madam C. J. Walker (1867–1919), pictured on this badge, organized the Hair Culturalists Union of America. The badge belonged to Alice Gause, a participant in a Walker convention.

My great grandmother Rose
mother of Ashley gave her this sack when
she was sold at age 9 in South Carolina
it held a tattered dress 3 handfulls of
pecans a braid of Roses hair. Told her
It be filled with my Love always
she never saw her again
Ashley is my grandmother
Ruth Middleton
1921

About three thousand people in sixteen cities participated in the Treasures program. More than a few of them were eager to give objects to NMAAHC. If the new museum would be the best home for something, NMAAHC accepted the objects. In other cases, the Treasures specialists urged people to donate their heirlooms to a museum or historical society in their own community instead.

Going, going, GONE! NMAAHC also added to its collections by bidding on objects at auctions held online or live at auction houses. The several hundred items NMAAHC purchased at auction include photographs of black cowboys and a catcher's mitt that belonged to Brooklyn Dodger and Hall-of-Famer Roy "Campy" Campanella (1921–1993). This son of an African American woman and a Sicilian man was Major League Baseball's first black catcher.

Some of the things NMAAHC collected were found objects that cost nothing other than the time and energy of staffers such as the ones who descended on a Barack Obama

Curator Elaine Nicholas with a participant at the NMAAHC Treasures program in Charleston, South Carolina. Looking on are Museum Director Lonnie Bunch (left), South Carolina Representative James Clyburn (center), and Deputy Director Kinshasha Conwill (right). Various workaday items, including a lantern, a ladle, old-fashioned irons, and wrenches, were brought in.

Right: A signed banner from the Obama campaign office in Columbia, Missouri, features one of the 2008 campaign slogans.

BRING U.S. TOGETHER

VOTE **CHISHOLM** 1972
UNBOUGHT AND UNBOSSED

campaign office in Fairfax, Virginia, shortly after his historic election to the presidency in 2008. Their haul of about a hundred items included furniture, strategy boards, and campaign materials printed in multiple languages.

After six years of seeking, searching, and sorting donations and acquisitions, NMAAHC had about twenty thousand artifacts by the end of 2013. Among the smallest was a centuries-old amulet of shackles. Members of the Lobi tribe in what is now Ghana wore this bronze charm as protection against capture by slave traders.

By late 2013, the museum also had some of its largest items—some so big they had to be lowered into the site while the museum was still under construction, because they would never fit through the front door, back door, or any other door after the building was completed.

One of those objects is Southern Railway car no. 1200. Built in 1922, this roughly 155,000-pound,

NMAAHC acquired historical and modern objects through its program "Save Our African American Treasures," including (left) this carte-de-visite of a woman and a young boy (1865); (center) an admissions ticket to the "Colored Balcony" of a segregated movie theater in Leesville, Louisiana (1950s); and (above) a 1972 presidential campaign poster for candidate Congresswoman Shirley Chisholm (1924–2005), a Brooklynite whose father was born in Guyana and her mother in Barbados.

Left: This tiny amulet was forged sometime in the 1600s or 1700s. It's less than two inches across.

Southern Railway car no. 1200 before its eighteen-month refurbishment by electricians, metalworkers, painters, and other skilled people in Stearns, Kentucky. Southern Railway operated in Florida, Georgia, Kentucky, and Tennessee.

80-foot-long passenger coach was outfitted according to Jim Crow laws, with separate and very unequal racial sections. The front, "white" section took up nearly two-thirds of the train and had larger lounges and restrooms than those found in the "colored" section.

When NMAAHC visitors move through this train car, they see with their own eyes and feel with their own hearts what it was like to live Jim Crow. They see and feel the humiliation black people endured en route to visit a friend, start college, or attend a loved one's funeral. Visitors also tap into how segregation could bind and damage white people, as it fostered the notion of white superiority and white entitlement and cut them off from other human beings who loved like them, laughed like them, and had much to offer.

While NMAAHC was building its collection, it was also raising money to support these acquisitions and erect a building to house them, and for a host of other things a museum needs to function. One major donor was media mogul Oprah Winfrey. In 2007 she gave the museum $1 million, then, six years later, a whopping $12 million.

Winfrey's donation was a thunderclap, but equally meaningful were the donations from people without fistfuls of dollars, like an elderly black shoeshine man Director Bunch met in the airport in Austin, Texas.

"You're that Washington, you know, museum guy on TV?" asked the man as he worked.

"Yes," Bunch replied.

His shoes shined, Bunch handed the man his payment. The elderly black man told Bunch to keep the six dollars for the museum. "Because if you do this museum right," he said, "my grandchildren will finally understand what I did to life and what life did to me."

Of course a major part of doing the museum "right" is creating just the right home for it.

BUILD *a* FITTING HOME

"The choice of design for the Smithsonian's new National Museum of African American History and Culture may well be the highest-profile architectural decision that will be made in Washington for years to come."

—*The Washington Post*, April 7, 2009

Round, square, or another geometric shape? Should it be made of stone or brick? Metal or marble? And what about the building's look? Sleek and ultra-modern? Or should it echo something ancient?

Before NMAAHC could even think about design questions like these, there was a lot of preliminary work to be done. Environmental impact studies compiled historical and natural science information about the site to identify buried water, electrical, and other utility lines, which would need to be rerouted or capped. The museum also had to get up to speed on the mandates of the Noise Control, Clean Air, and Clean Water Acts. The District of Columbia Historic Preservation Office weighed in, because the site was part of the Washington Monument Grounds and the National Mall. The National Capital Planning Commission, the National Park Service, and the U.S. Commission of Fine Arts were consulted on a range of issues, too. On top of that, the public was given a chance to ask questions and express opinions in open town hall meetings.

NMAAHC rising, May 5, 2015.

In July 2008, the Smithsonian issued a Request for Qualifications inviting teams of architects and engineers (A/E) from around the world to submit their qualifications to design a museum of approximately 350,000 square feet.

A/E teams include building designers, lighting designers, landscape architects, IT and acoustics experts, and structural, civil, geotechnical, mechanical, and electrical engineers. The A/E teams chosen for the next stage, the design competition, could present their ideas via 3-D models, schematics, renderings—however they saw fit. Naturally they would have to provide loads of details, from the construction budget to the construction schedule. By law, NMAAHC could cost no more than $500 million (half provided by the federal government, half raised by the museum). Energy efficiency was another must: NMAAHC would be the first "green" building on the Mall.

And there were two major, major musts! The design had to show sensitivity to the site's surroundings, most especially to the Washington Monument, which stands 700 yards away. It also had to reflect an appreciation and understanding of black history and culture.

Twenty-two A/E teams met the challenge and submitted their designs by the September 19, 2008, deadline.

The sculpture by Yoruban crafts-man Olowe of Ise (circa 1873–1938) that inspired architect David Adjaye of the Freelon Adjaye Bond/ SmithGroup (FABS).

Right: Adjaye's sketches of the museum showing the Yoruban influence.

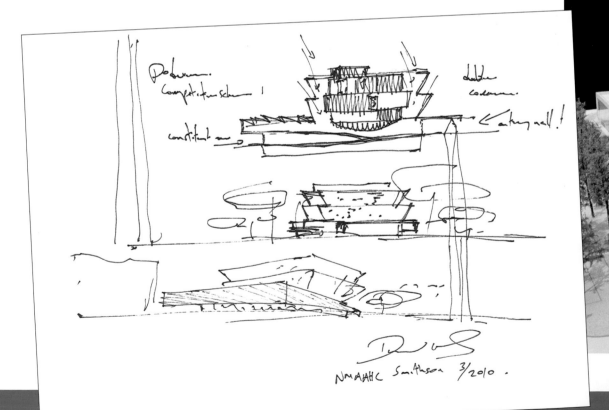

The Smithsonian chose six finalists and then on April 14, 2009, announced the winner: a four-firm team known as the Freelon Adjaye Bond/SmithGroup (FABS).

FABS's central design feature was a corona atop a stone plinth or platform. This corona was inspired by the top sections of late nineteenth- and early twentieth-century Yoruban sculptures, which were used as architectural columns. The Yoruba are one of the largest ethnic groups in West and West Central Africa, birthplace of most of the millions of African children and adults targeted for enslavement in Europe and the Americas.

The museum's corona, which can also be seen as an upside-down pyramid (another design concept out of Africa), also acknowledges the pyramid-capped Washington Monument.

Team members of FABS, from left: Hal David, Peter Cook, NMAAHC Director Lonnie Bunch, David Adjaye, Phil Freelon, and then Secretary of the Smithsonian G. Wayne Clough.

Left: FABS's winning design.

"Celebration and praise" were uppermost on FABS's mind, said lead designer-architect David Adjaye. Certain that, in its collections and exhibits, NMAAHC would never downplay the terrors and tortures people of African descent have endured on America's shores, FABS wanted the building to project triumph. "Our scheme

is quite soaring from the interiors. The space suggests uplift," explained Phil Freelon, the project's executive architect. FABS envisioned that the corona would appear to be levitating, in keeping with the spirit of celebration, praise, and uplift.

The exterior of the building would have a shimmering bronze-colored filigree envelope or skin: an homage to black ironworkers, enslaved and free, who designed and forged thousands of fences, gates, and other decorative metal for mansions and public buildings in New Orleans, Louisiana, and Charleston, South Carolina, in the 1800s and 1900s.

As the museum moved from concept to construction, the design was modified and fine-tuned. Materials were changed, dimensions were changed. As for that stone-clad plinth, it was done away with altogether. Instead the building's base became a glass box with a porch floating over the main entrance. And the corona? It soared from two tiers to three.

Nine years after the dream got its wings, at last, at last, on February 22, 2012, George Washington's birthday, the ground-breaking ceremony took place for the National Museum of African American History and Culture, the Smithsonian's nineteenth museum. This momentous event was held in a huge heated tent. Distinguished guests included President Barack Obama; First

Top: Iron grillwork in New Orleans.

Bottom: Architectural image of the museum's reflecting pool.

Right: While the design was being refined, other equally important work was being done—choosing a builder, for one. In July 2011, the Smithsonian selected the three-firm general contracting team of Clark/Smoot/Russell.

Lady Michelle Obama; former First Lady Laura Bush; former Secretary of State General Colin Powell; Washington's mayor, Vincent Gray; and two politicians who sponsored the bill that gave the dream wings back in 2003, Georgia Representative John Lewis and former Kansas senator and then governor Sam Brownback.

"Today, in the words of Washington, DC, poet Lewis Alexander, we call the lost dream back," said NMAAHC Director Lonnie Bunch, welcoming some six hundred guests. "Today we begin to make manifest on this Mall, on this sacred space, the dreams of many generations who fought for and believed that there should be a site in the nation's capital that will help all Americans remember and honor African American history and culture."

Congressman John Lewis, who had championed the museum for more than twenty years, was equally arresting. "What we are witnessing today will go down in history," he said. "It is the substance of things hoped for and the validation of our dreams. It is the moment a people protested, struggled, and longed for. It is the moment millions of our ancestors believed in, but died never to behold."

Confident that NMAAHC would be a ready force for good and enlightenment for all people, Lewis looked forward to the day when he would be able to "amble through the exhibits, search through the archives, participate in the programs, rest my tired feet in the café, and get lost in history inside the granite walls of an idea whose time has finally come."

Top: First Lady Michelle Obama looks on lovingly as President Obama embraces John Lewis after his speech. "This day has been a long time coming," said the president when he addressed the crowd.

Bottom: The ceremonial groundbreaking inside that big tent on February 22, 2012. Left to right: Richard Parsons, senior advisor to Providence Equity and co-chair of NMAAHC's council (advisory board); Patty Stonesifer, a member of the Smithsonian Board of Regents and its former chair; Laura Bush, former First Lady and NMAAHC council member; Wayne Clough, Secretary of the Smithsonian Institution at the time; Lonnie Bunch, NMAAHC director; Richard Kurin, the Smithsonian's Under Secretary for History, Art, and Culture; France Córdova, chair of the Smithsonian Board of Regents; and Linda Johnson Rice, chair of Johnson Publishing Company and co-chair of NMAAHC's council.

NMAAHC *construction site in*
mid-2013.

Shortly after the groundbreaking, construction began for real.

Talk about a big dig! Construction workers tunneled 80 feet down below ground level to lay the museum's foundation, making NMAAHC the deepest museum on the Mall. Why? More than half the museum would be underground, to keep it from blocking certain views of the Washington Monument and obstructing sight lines along the Mall.

Since this building would have five stories below ground and five above, construction crews spent months excavating more than 300,000 cubic yards of packed dirt, then grading (leveling out) the base. While that was under way, an earth retention system—aka a cave-in prevention system—was built. Pile drivers drilled steel I-beams into the ground along the perimeter

Pouring cement and working on the museum's foundation.

of the big dig, inserted lagging (heavy wood boards) behind the piles at intervals, then welded them into place.

Mounds and mounds of dirt wasn't all that had to be removed. The NMAAHC site is located at a low point on the Mall, which means ground water drains into it. At one point construction crews were pumping out about 85 gallons of water a minute. After two months of pumping and draining, workers started in on sheeting and shoring. They built water-blocking walls, also known as slurry walls.

In November 2012, work on the museum's foundation got under way. That included pouring 55,000 cubic yards of concrete for the museum's footings (or base) and for its 60-foot high, 6-foot-thick foundation walls. Establishing a foundation to last for the ages also involved erecting four massive cores to support the museum.

Work on the museum continued for days, months, years. It took more than two years to construct the aboveground concrete-and-steel superstructure—mission accomplished in January 2015. By April, the museum's glass casing was complete and workers started installing the first of the corona's 3,600 bronze-colored panels.

NMAAHC in September 2015. Landscape architect Catherine Gustafson oversaw the design of the museum's five acres.

Right: The first of the corona's bronze-colored panels was installed on April 14, 2015.

While the building's exterior was taking shape and form, so was its interior, which includes 86,000 square feet of permanent exhibition space on different floors and a large gallery for temporary exhibits, along with areas for public programs, the 350-seat Oprah Winfrey Theater, a café, and a gift shop. The museum also needed a bunch of behind-the-scenes rooms, from collections workrooms and exhibit production shops to administrative offices. Of course, all these rooms and spaces had to be outfitted with equipment, then adorned with fixtures and furnishings. And let's not forget the museum's "guts," such as utility cables, duct work, piping, heating and cooling systems, and mechanisms that make elevators and escalators function. Then there was the landscaping to see to, which includes intimate groups of trees and reading groves, seating areas reflecting three themes: spirituality, optimism and hope, and resiliency. Building a museum takes a lot of work!

Constructing NMAAHC took the sweat and muscle, the skills and smarts of more than four hundred men and women: engineers and electricians, pile drivers and plumbers, carpenters and crane operators, along with a host of other skilled and unskilled laborers. And there were managers for this, managers for that.

Derek Ross (center), Deputy Director, Construction Division, Smithsonian's Office of Facilities, gives a tour of the building in progress.

The museum's builders included McKissack & McKissack, an African American–owned construction management firm. For the company's founder, Deryl McKissack, working on NMAAHC was a very deep and moving thing, for she is a descendant of Moses McKissack (1790–1865), a member of the Asante tribe who became a master builder while enslaved in North Carolina. "If you think about it, fifty years ago," said a McKissack & McKissack's VP, Lisa Anders, "we weren't able to sit at the same lunch counter [as white people]. [Being] on this particular project has a lot of significance for us."

Another proud member of the museum's building team was Lonnie Locke, a black pile driver. Locke looked forward to taking his young son to the museum when it opened, so he could say, "I built that!" of a monumental place that took thirteen years to erect but one hundred years to come about.

A monumental place for important research, lively presentations, innovative programs, and interactive experiences.

A monumental place to showcase plays, dance, and song.

A monumental place to hold galas and other special events.

Above all, when Lonnie Locke's son enters NMAAHC, he will be entering a treasure trove of artifacts that bear witness to the black sojourn in America over the course of hundreds of years. He will be entering a place where the mind can explore and the spirit soar.

You can enter this magnificent museum right now. Just turn the page.

WELCOME *the* WORLD

"Whether your family's been in this country two hundred years or twenty minutes . . . I want you to come to this museum and say, 'I get it. This is not a black story. This is my story. This is the American story.'"

—Lonnie Bunch, January 2009

Exactly what would people experience once inside NMAAHC? Long before construction got under way, Director Bunch, Deputy Director Conwill, and NMAAHC project management directors, curators, and other staffers brainstormed what the museum's inaugural exhibitions should be. Members of the team met with people from the community and toured the country to get input as to how NMAAHC should tell the story of the African American experience. And this became their guiding principle: to enrich visitors' knowledge and understanding of people more than events. "We want to bring everything to a human scale," Bunch told a reporter in October 2014. "Rather than coming and saying you've learned about slavery, you'll say, 'I've learned about people who went through that experience.'"

Team NMAAHC decided on eleven permanent exhibitions, organized around three themes: history, community, culture.

In November 2015, "Commemorate and Celebrate Freedom," a stirring video by filmmaker Stanley J. Nelson and co-producer Marcia Smith, was projected on the exterior of the nearly complete museum. The powerful words and images shown honored the anniversaries of the end of the Civil War; the Thirteenth Amendment, which abolished slavery; and the Voting Rights Act of 1965.

SLAVERY *and* FREEDOM

What role did slavery play in the making of America? What was daily life like for enslaved men and women? For their children? What was it like to be a free black person during the days of slavery? How is it that America, a nation pledged to "Life, Liberty, and the pursuit of Happiness," approved of so shameful a thing as slavery for more than two hundred years? The exhibition *Slavery and Freedom* addresses these questions and more with its wide array of artifacts. Some objects speak to the horrors of slavery. Others to resistance and triumphs.

A lithograph (print) from 1870 celebrating passage of the Fifteenth Amendment, which granted African American men the right to vote.

THE FIFTEENTH AMENDMENT.

Frederick Douglass (1818–1895), the famous abolitionist and statesman who was once enslaved, endorsed this flyer (1863) to encourage black men to fight for the Union during the Civil War.

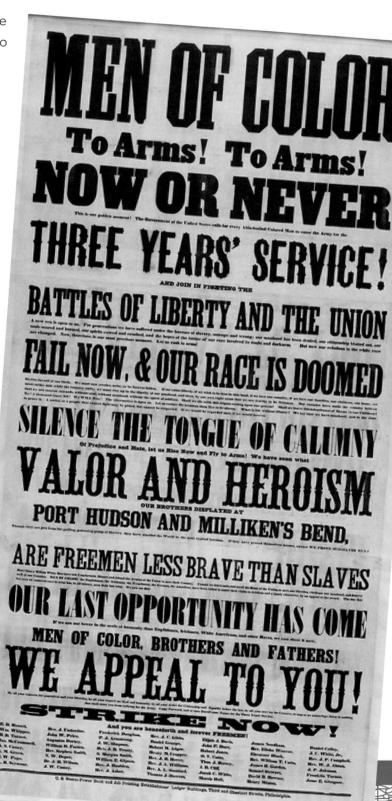

Frontispiece and title page of the first full-length autobiography of a once-enslaved man (1837 edition shown). Originally published in 1789, the book was a bestseller in its author's lifetime. Olaudah Equiano (1745–1797) was also *known as Gustavus Vassa. Though he claimed that he was born in Africa, he may in fact have been born in South Carolina.

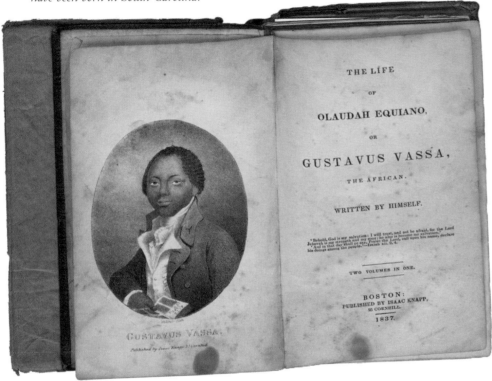

An 1838 watercolor painting by Lieutenant Henry Samuel Hawker (1816–1889) of the Portuguese slave ship Diligenté captured with six hundred enslaved Africans on board.

Advertisement for an auction of ten enslaved families, 1855.

Joseph Trammell (1831–1859)'s Certificate of Freedom No. 1952, stored in a handmade tin box (1852), shows this Virginian was a free black man, not a fugitive or enslaved.

A gunpowder horn for Prince Simbo (1750–1810), a black patriot who served as a private in Connecticut's Seventh Regiment during the American Revolution. An inscription on the gunpowder horn reads: "Prince Simbo his horn made at Glastonbury November 17th AD 1777."

DEFENDING FREEDOM, DEFINING FREEDOM: *the* ERA *of* SEGREGATION

In a journey from the end of Reconstruction in 1877 through the Civil Rights movement of the 1960s, visitors here learn about key aspects of the ongoing struggle by African Americans—and the nation at large—to define and make real the meaning of freedom. This exhibition explores how African Americans survived challenges and setbacks while crafting important roles for themselves as full-fledged citizens. It also shows how the United States itself changed as a consequence of black strivings and victories. Some of the most powerful artifacts in the museum are located here.

Front and back of a National Negro Business League badge, circa 1908. Pictured is Booker T. Washington (1856–1915), head of Tuskegee Institute (now University) in Tuskegee, Alabama. Washington, born into slavery, founded the National Negro Business League in 1900 to promote black entrepreneurship.

Fisk Jubilee Singers (circa 1872). Formed in 1871, this choral group traveled the world raising funds for their school, Fisk University in Nashville, Tennessee. The cover of this 1883 book about the singers by J. B. T. Marsh features Fisk's Jubilee Hall, built with money earned by the singers.

WAITING ROOM
(INTERSTATE AND WHITE INTRASTATE PASSENGERS)

Sign from a segregated bus station in Birmingham, Alabama (circa 1957).

A 1966 pamphlet for the Lowndes County Freedom Organization, known as the Black Panther Party because of its logo. This Alabama independent political party inspired the Black Panther Party for Self-Defense organized in Oakland, California, in October 1966.

As Appeal to You from

JAMES FARMER
Congress of Racial Equality

MARTIN LUTHER KING, JR.
Southern Christian Leadership Conference

JOHN LEWIS
Student Non-violent Coordinating Committee

A. PHILIP RANDOLPH
Negro American Labor Council

ROY WILKINS
National Association for the Advancement of Colored People

WHITNEY YOUNG
National Urban League

to MARCH on
WASHINGTON
WEDNESDAY AUGUST 28, 1963

America faces a crisis . . .
Millions of Negroes are denied freedom . . .
Millions of citizens, black and white, are unemployed . . .

We demand:
— Meaningful Civil Rights Laws
— Massive Federal Works Program
— Full and Fair Employment
— Decent Housing
— The Right to Vote
— Adequate Integrated Education

In our community, groups and individuals are mobilizing for the August 28th demonstration. For information regarding your participation, call the local Coordinating Committee for the

MARCH ON WASHINGTON
FOR JOBS AND FREEDOM

1417 You Street, N.W.

ADams 2-2320

CO-CHAIRMEN

...ter E. Fauntroy, Coordinator
. Beavers
...les Brown

Edward A. Hailes
Julius W. Hobson
Sterling Tucker

Two stools from the whites-only lunch counter at Woolworth's five-and-dime store in Greensboro, North Carolina. On February 1, 1960, four black college students sat down at this counter and ordered coffee. They were not served—but they refused to budge in protest of the store's racist policy. The Greensboro sit-ins, which lasted for six months, inspired a national wave of sit-ins and boycotts at other whites-only establishments, as well as wade-ins at segregated pools and beaches. These actions helped desegregate Woolworth's and other places and inspired a youth-led movement for civil rights.

A flyer from the historic March on Washington for Jobs and Freedom held on the National Mall on August 28, 1963. Roughly 250,000 people turned out for this protest for justice, where Reverend Dr. Martin Luther King Jr. delivered his "I Have a Dream" speech. Other speakers included future Georgia congressman John Lewis.

CHANGING AMERICA: 1968 *and* BEYOND

An estimated 750,000 black women turned out for the 1997 Million Woman March promoting unity and community. Two years earlier, the Million Man March was held in Washington, DC, on the National Mall.

From the Black Power movement to the growing black middle class, from the hip-hop revolution to the age of Obama, this exhibition looks at the state of black America in the decades after the assassination of Reverend Dr. Martin Luther King Jr. on April 4, 1968, in Memphis, Tennessee.

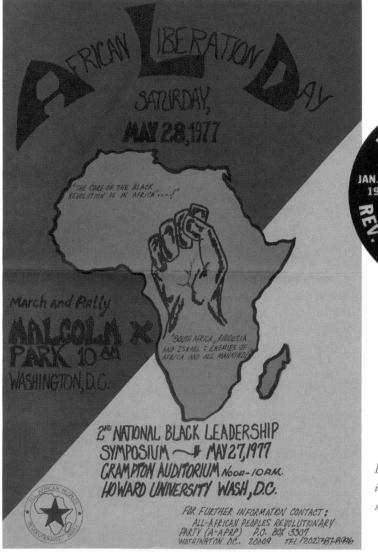

Poster for an African Liberation Day event in Washington, DC (1977). This international annual event started in the 1950s and was created to protest the subjugation of people of African descent all over the world.

Political memorabilia from the 1960s through 2008: three buttons feature icons Martin Luther King Jr. (1929–1968), Malcolm X (1925–1965), and Barbara Jordan (1936–1996), the first black female Texas state senator and first black congresswoman from the Deep South.

MAKING a WAY OUT of NO WAY

This exhibition celebrates the fact that era after era, black people devised ways to defy oppression and overcome obstacles. As the saying goes, they steadfastly "made a way out of no way"—turning don't to done, can't to can. They did this through religious and civic organizations, through educational institutions, through a multitude of other networks, and by establishing their own businesses. And community worked!

The motto of the National Association of Colored Women's Clubs (NACWC) on a banner (circa 1924) of the Oklahoma Federation of Colored Women. NACWC was formed in 1896 as an umbrella organization for local and regional black women's organizations.

Harlem Better Business League poster (circa 1940).

A photographic postcard of people outside a church (place and date unknown). The black church has always played a key role in the political, social, economic, educational, and spiritual uplift of people of African descent in the United States.

A 1968 issue of Negro Digest, founded by John H. Johnson (1918–2005), one of the twentieth century's most successful black entrepreneurs. His other endeavors included Jet and Ebony magazines.

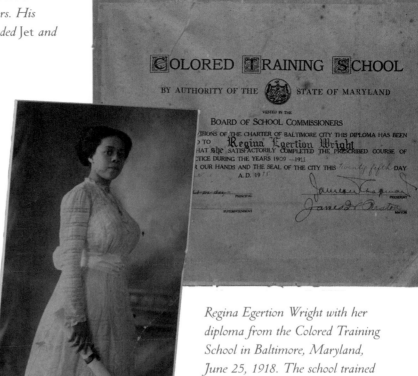

Regina Egertion Wright with her diploma from the Colored Training School in Baltimore, Maryland, June 25, 1918. The school trained elementary school teachers.

A desk from the Hope Rosenwald School near Pomaria, South Carolina. This two-room elementary school served thousands of black children from 1926 until 1954. It was one of the more than five thousand schools for black students built in the rural South in the early 1900s, funded in part by local communities and in part by the Rosenwald Fund established by the Jewish millionaire Julius Rosenwald (1862–1932). Rosenwald helped build these schools at the request of Booker T. Washington. Local groups contributed money and often land, building material, and labor.

POWER of PLACE

The displays in another Community exhibition explore an essential question: How does place shape people—and how do people shape a place? *Power of Place* provides an in-depth look at ten distinct places. Together they speak to the diversity of the black experience in different parts of the nation and during different periods of time. These places include Lyles Station, a small community on Indiana's southern border established by blacks in the early 1800s; Oak Bluffs on Martha's Vineyard, Massachusetts, where blacks have lived since the seventeenth century and where well-to-do blacks have had vacation homes since the early 1900s; Chicago, Illinois, a mecca for African Americans eager to shake the Southern dust from their feet, escape racism, and seek better lives and opportunities during the Great Migration of the early and mid-twentieth century.

At the movies in Chicago, Illinois, in 1941.

Children on the beach at Oak Bluffs on Martha's Vineyard (1922).

Guests outside Oak Bluffs' first black-owned inn, Shearer Cottage (1931).

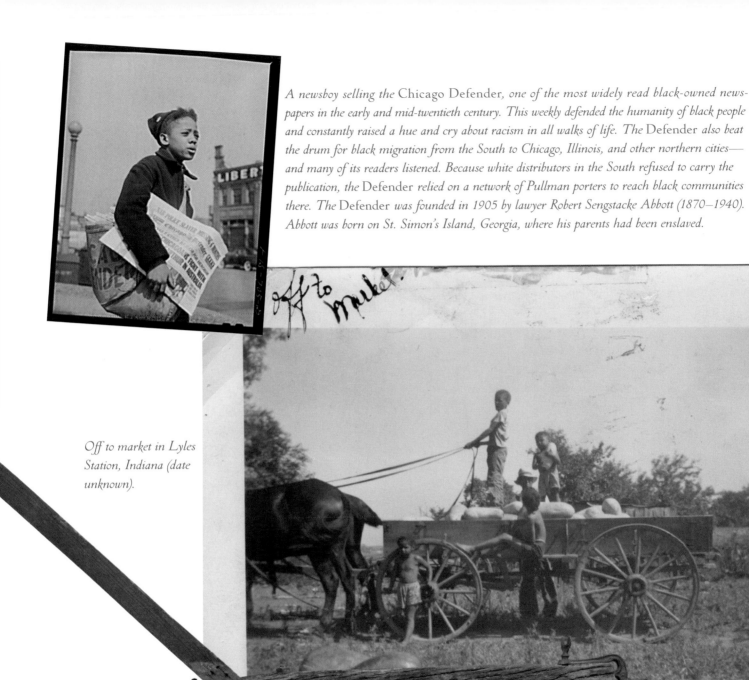

A newsboy selling the Chicago Defender, one of the most widely read black-owned newspapers in the early and mid-twentieth century. This weekly defended the humanity of black people and constantly raised a hue and cry about racism in all walks of life. The Defender also beat the drum for black migration from the South to Chicago, Illinois, and other northern cities— and many of its readers listened. Because white distributors in the South refused to carry the publication, the Defender relied on a network of Pullman porters to reach black communities there. The Defender was founded in 1905 by lawyer Robert Sengstacke Abbott (1870–1940). Abbott was born on St. Simon's Island, Georgia, where his parents had been enslaved.

Off to market in Lyles Station, Indiana (date unknown).

A twentieth-century walking plow from Lyles Station.

SPORTS: LEVELING *the* PLAYING FIELD

This exhibition on the world of sports is hardly just about fun and games. Through much of the nation's history, African Americans were denied the chance to compete at the highest levels. Black athletic achievements have long been part and parcel of the push for social justice. The *Sports: Leveling the Playing Field* exhibition tells this story from the days of slavery up to the present.

Track-and-field champion Carl Lewis won four gold medals at the 1984 Summer Olympics in Los Angeles, California, including this one for the men's long jump; a pair of his running shoes.

A leotard worn by gymnast Gabby Douglas in 2003. She won a team gold medal at the 2012 Summer Olympics in London, England, and became the first African American gymnast in Olympics history to win the individual All-Around Champion gold medal. Also shown: a ticket to the 2012 Olympics.

Black Sports magazine, April 1971. On the cover are Kareem Abdul Jabbar (left), the NBA's all-time leading scorer, and Oscar Robertson (right).

BLACK SPORTS

APRIL 1971 50 CENTS

Oscar and Lew: NBA's Winning Buck$

Matt Snell's Recovery Toss-up

Chamberlain Speaks Out

Mississippi Sports Revolution

Willye White's Fifth Team

NFL's Buddy Young

Rappin' with John Carlos & Willie Davis

SPECIAL: Johnny Sample's Confessions of a Dirty Ballplayer

EXCLUSIVE: Ron Johnson's Own Story

Basketball signed by Magic Johnson and Larry Bird, members of the "Dream Team," the US men's basketball team that won the gold medal at the 1992 Summer Olympics in Barcelona, Spain. The team also included Patrick Ewing and Michael Jordan.

A bat from the 1965 All-Star Game, signed by Hall-of-Fame center fielder Willie Mays. Mays was with the San Francisco Giants at the time.

Pennant for the October 30, 1974, "Rumble in the Jungle" boxing match held in a soccer stadium in Kinshasa, Zaire (now Democratic Republic of the Congo). The challenger, Muhammad Ali, beat champ George Foreman by knockout in round eight.

Cleveland Brown's football jersey (circa 1965) worn and signed by NFL great Jim Brown, one of football's most famous fullbacks.

Althea Gibson (1927–2003) was the first black tennis player allowed to compete in the US National Championships (1950) and at Wimbledon (1951). She later became the first African American to win each of these important championships. This photo is from 1957.

Martin Stadium, Memphis, Tennessee, one of the few African American owned and operated ballparks. Ball players from far right to left: Jackie Robinson (1919–1972) broke the color barrier in Major League Baseball on April 15, 1947, when he stepped onto Ebbets Field as a Brooklyn Dodger; Cleveland Indian Larry Doby (1923–2003), MLB's second black player (July 1947); seated, Ernie Banks (1931–2015), then with the Kansas City Monarchs, a Negro Leagues team, and later the first black player for the Chicago Cubs. This photograph was taken in 1953 by legendary African American photojournalist Ernest C. Withers (1922–2007).

An early 1950s catcher's mitt that belonged to baseball great Roy Campanella.

DOUBLE VICTORY:
the AFRICAN AMERICAN MILITARY EXPERIENCE

Another Community exhibition is equally absorbing as it chronicles black valor in war from the American Revolution on: service for country during slavery; service for country when citizenship was denied; service for country when Jim Crow reigned; and service for country after blacks were given more opportunities to rise through the ranks. *Double Victory: The African American Military Experience* also reminds you that black men and women who served in America's armed forces often did so hoping both to better themselves and to gain more respect for their community at large.

Cornelius H. Charlton (1929–1951), a sergeant in the US Army's 24th Infantry Regiment, was awarded the Purple Heart in the Korean War (1950–1953) posthumously along with this Medal of Honor, the US military's highest decoration.

A 1943 US Treasury poster featuring distinguished Tuskegee Airman Lieutenant Robert W. Diez (1919–1992). During World War II (1939–1945) Diez shot down two enemy planes in Italy.

Front and back of the Congressional Gold Medal awarded in 2007 to the Tuskegee Airmen, the first black pilots in the US armed forces.

Pauline Cookman in military uniform, circa 1945.

A voucher for Jack Little to be paid thirteen pounds, six shillings, and eight pence for service in the Continental Army during the American Revolution (1775–1783). Little, a resident of New Haven, Connecticut, served from 1779 to 1783. His pay order was issued in Hartford on June 1, 1782.

A helmet (circa 1917) belonging to Peter L. Robinson Sr. (1892–1979), who served in World War I (1914–1918).

An ambrotype (photograph on glass) of a soldier in the Civil War (1861–1865).

Troop A, Ninth US Cavalry, on horseback during the Spanish-American War (1898).

A small late nineteenth-century carte-de-visite shows a sailor identified only as "Jim."

THE CULTURE GALLERIES

NMAAHC offers four exhibitions that focus on different cultural aspects. *Cultural Expressions* asks, What is black culture? then provides answers by exploring such things as body language and adornment, food and foodways, and arts and crafts. *Taking the Stage* celebrates the contributions people of African descent have made to American culture on stage, in films, and on TV. *Musical Crossroads* takes you on a journey into the wide world of music in which blacks have made a mark—sacred and secular, music with roots in Africa and Europe and elsewhere in the world. When you reach *Visual Arts*, you'll find stunning treasures, including works on canvas, works on paper, sculpture, ceramics, mixed media, and art made out of found objects.

Chuck Berry's 1959 Gibson ES-350T electric guitar. Berry is an influential music pioneer and "Father of Rock 'n' Roll." In 1986, he was among the first people inducted into the Rock and Roll Hall of Fame.

Ghana Women Dancing *(1968), oil on canvas by painter, muralist, sculptor, and illustrator John Biggers (1924–2001). These and other depictions of African life are rooted in Bigger's life-changing trip to West Africa in 1957.*

These satin-and-leather pointe shoes (circa 2006) graced the feet of Lauren Anderson, an acclaimed dancer with the Houston Ballet. In 1990 Anderson made history when she became the first black principal ballerina of a major American ballet company.

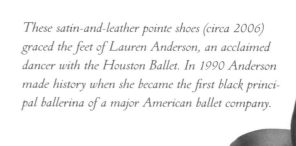

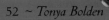

A poster (1899) for the famed soprano and actress Mattie Wilkes (circa 1876–1927).

Playbill for the 1975–1979 Broadway production of The Wiz, directed by Trinidadian Geoffrey Holder (1930–2014) and starring Stephanie Mills.

The costume designed by Geoffrey Holder for Glinda, the Good Witch of the South, in the 1975 Broadway musical production The Wiz, a spin on The Wizard of Oz with an all-black cast.

The famous black fedora of the "King of Pop" Michael Jackson (1958–2009), which he wore on his 1984 "Victory Tour." Jackson won thirteen Grammys over the course of his career.

A painted plaster sculpture Ethiopia (1921) by Meta Vaux Warrick Fuller (1877–1968), who studied in Europe with the great French sculptor Auguste Rodin.

A Selmer trumpet (circa 1946) that belonged to Louis Armstrong (1901–1971), the legendary musician, singer, bandleader, and actor known as Satchmo.

More than one hundred years ago, in a speech in Baltimore, Maryland, in 1877, Frederick Douglass suggested that every American should visit the nation's capital at least once. Were he alive today, Douglass would no doubt say the same thing about Smithsonian's National Museum of African American History and Culture.

It's an experience like no other.

FACTS *and* FIGURES

406,000 square feet: total area of the museum

105,000 square feet: exhibition space (almost twice the area of the White House)

70,000 square feet: area of the corona's cast aluminum panels

245 tons: weight of the corona's cast aluminum panels

55,000 cubic yards: volume of concrete (more than enough to fill the National Mall's Reflecting Pool)

320,000 cubic yards: volume of dirt excavated and hauled from the site

32,000: number of trucks used to haul dirt from the site. (Lined up, that would be 151 miles of truck, enough to go around the National Mall 35 times.)

2,500 tons: weight of structural steel

77 feet: height of corona (more than twice the depth of the Washington Monument foundation)

70 feet: portion of the museum below grade (a couple of feet more than the White House South Facade); 60 percent of the total building is below the ground

Acknowledgments

Sheila Keenan, one of the hardest-working women in publishing—if not the hardest-working—thank you for your marvelous sense and sensibilities and top-notch author care. Janet Pascal, executive production editor, what a great pleasure (and privilege) to work with you (and your intelligence) again. Associate production editor Krista Ahlberg, I thank you for your sharp eyes and attention to detail. Kate Renner, designer—what a marvelous designing mind you have. Thank you, Ellen Nanney and Sharon C. Park with the Smithsonian Institution, for your assists on several fronts. And bless you, team NMAAHC.

PHOTO CREDITS Every effort has been made to identify and properly credit copyright holders. All rights reserved.

Art © John T. Biggers Estate/Licensed by VAGA, New York, NY: 52 top right; gift of Gerald and Anita Smith • Bridgeman Images: 28 left, photo © by Heini Schneebeli • Department of Special Collections and University Archives, W. E. B. Du Bois Library, University of Massachusetts Amherst: 5 top • Gibson® Brands, Inc.: 52 bottom left • International Olympic Committee: 48 left; 48 top right • Karchmer, Alan: 54–55 • Library of Congress, Prints and Photographs Division: 4 top; 7 top; 30 top; 38 left; 46 top; 47 top • Lyles Station Historic Preservation Corporation: 47 right • Office of Congressman John Lewis: 7 bottom, photo by J. D. Scott • Playbill, Inc.: 53 top right • Shearer Cottage: 46 bottom left; 46 bottom right • Smithsonian Facilities: 28 right; 29 top; 35 • Smithsonian Institution Archives: iv; 2; 8; 9; 10; 13; 14 top; 16; 20 bottom; 21 bottom left; 22 top; 25; 26; 30 bottom right; 31; 32; 33; 34; 36 • Smithsonian's National Museum of African American History and Culture: 4 bottom center; 4 bottom right; 6 bottom; 14 bottom; 15 left center; 20 top; 23 bottom; 30 bottom left; 38; 39 top; 39 bottom left; 39 bottom center; 40; 41 bottom left; 41 bottom right; 42 top right; 42 center right; 42 bottom right; 43 top left; 43 bottom left; 43 right; 44; 45 top right; 45 center; 48 bottom; 49 left; 49 top right; 49 center right; 49 bottom right; 50 left; 50 center; 50 bottom right; 51 top left; 51 top right; 51 bottom left; 51 bottom right; 53 center; 53 bottom center; 54–55 • Smithsonian's National Museum of African American History and Culture, gifts: 4 bottom left, Liljenquist Family Collection; 5 bottom, Bobbie Ross; 15 right,

Juanita Evangeline Moore, Skip Pagan, and Darren Pagan; 18 top left, 18 bottom left, Charles L. Blockson; 18 top right, Garrison Family; 18 bottom center, Ginette DePreist; 19 Black Fashion Museum; 21 top, 21 bottom, Dr. Patricia Heaston; 22 bottom, Mid-Missouri Campaign Field Office; 23 top left, Linda and Artis Cason; 23 top center, David A. Lowrance; 23 top right, Ellen Brooks; 24, Pete Claussen and Gulf and Ohio Railways; 39 top left, William E. West Sr. and Family; 39 left, 39 center, Elaine E. Thompson; 41 top, University of Mary Washington; 41 bottom left, International Civil Rights Center & Museum; 42 left, Catherine M. Bailey; 42 bottom right, Abiodun and Last Poets Memorabilia; 43 left, 43 center, Dawn Simon Spears and Alvin Spears Sr.; 43 bottom, M. Denise Dennis; 45 top left, © 1968 Johnson Publishing Company, Inc; 45 bottom left, Hope School Community Center; 47 center, Lyles Station Historic Preservation Corporation; 48 left, Gabrielle Douglas; 48 top right, Carl Lewis Estate; 49 bottom center, © Black Sports Magazine; 49 center, 49 left, Donald Felder and Family; 50 top right, Ray R. and Patricia A. D. Charlton; 51 center, Peter L. Robinson Jr. and Marie Robinson Johnson; 52 left, Charles E. Berry; 52 bottom, Lauren Anderson; 53 top left, Stephen and Catherine Markardt; 53 bottom left, Fuller Family, © Meta Vaux Warrick Fuller; 53 top right, Kayla Deigh Owens; 53 bottom right, Black Fashion Museum • Smithsonian National Museum of American History, Archives Center: 6 top; 12; 18 bottom right • Withers Family Trust: 49 bottom right, photo © Dr. Ernest C. Withers Sr.

VIKING
An imprint of Penguin Random House LLC
375 Hudson Street
New York, New York 10014

First published in the United States of America by Viking,
an imprint of Penguin Random House LLC, 2016

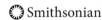 Smithsonian

SMITHSONIAN is a trademark owned by the Smithsonian Institution and is registered in the U.S. Patent and Trademark Office.

Smithsonian Enterprises:
Christopher Liedel, President
Carol LeBlanc, Senior Vice President, Education and Consumer Products
Brigid Ferraro, Vice President, Education and Consumer Products
Ellen Nanney, Licensing Manager
Kealy Gordon, Product Development Manager

This book would not have been possible without the entire NMAAHC staff and construction team, especially Director Lonnie Bunch, Deputy Director Kinshasha Holman Conwill, Renee S. Anderson, Amy Ballard, Michael Barnes, Jessica Brode, Laura Coyle, Williams Donnelly, Paul Gardullo, Emily Houf, Joanne Hyppolite, Alex Jamison, Cheryl Johnson, Donna Jones, Michèle Gates Moresi, Sharon Park, William Pretzer, Adam Rasmussen, Doug Remley, Marisa Russel, Deborah Scriber-Miller, Esther Washington, and Michelle Wilkinson.

LIBRARY OF CONGRESS CATALOGING-IN-PUBLICATION
Names: Bolden, Tonya, author.
Title: How to build a museum : Smithsonian's National Museum of African American History and Culture / Tonya Bolden.
Other titles: Smithsonian's National Museum of African American History and Culture
Description: New York : Viking Childrens Books, [2016] | Audience: Grades 4-6.
Identifiers: LCCN 2016011612 | ISBN 9780451476371 (hardcover)
Subjects: LCSH: National Museum of African American History and Culture
  (U.S.)—Juvenile literature. | African Americans—Museums—Washington
  (D.C.)—Juvenile literature. | Historical museums—Washington
  (D.C.)—Design and construction—Juvenile literature.
Classification: LCC E185.53 .B65 2016 | DDC 973/.0496073074—dc23
LC record available at http://lccn.loc.gov/2016011612

Set in Neutraface Slab Text   Designed by Kate Renner   Manufactured in China

10 9 8 7 6 5 4 3 2 1

NOTES

EPIGRAPHS

"History, as nearly . . .": James Baldwin, "The White Man's Guilt," *Ebony*, August 1965, p. 47.

"Dream Song": Langston Hughes and Arna Bontemps, eds., *The Poetry of the Negro, 1746–1949*. (Garden City, New York: Doubleday, 1949), p. 85.

DREAM

"The meeting of the Colored Citizens' . . .": "A Grand Reception to the Old Colored Veterans," *The Washington Bee*, June 19, 1915.

on the Encampment: "How the Parade Will Line Up Tomorrow," *Evening Star*, September 28, 1915, Part Two; Anna J. Greenlees, R.N. "The G.A.R. Encampment," *The American Journal of Nursing* Vol. 16, No. 2 (November 1915), p. 124; *Journal of the Forty-Ninth National Encampment Grand Army of the Republic* (Washington, DC: Government Printing Office, 1916), p. 252.

bill passage in 1929: "House Votes 248 to 86 For Negro Memorial," *New York Times*, March 3, 1929.

cost of milk in 1929: Stella Stewart and Faith M. Williams, "Retail Prices of Food 1923–1936," *Bulletin No. 635*, October 1937. (Washington, DC: Government Printing Office, 1938), Table 7, p. 85.

HAVE A VISION

"He is charged with . . .": DeNeed L. Brown, "Lonnie Bunch's Vision for the Museum of African American History and Culture," *Washington Post*, February 17, 2012. http://www.washingtonpost.com/lifestyle/style/lonnie-bunchs-vision-for-the-museum-of-african-american-history-and-culture/2012/02/06/gIQAffc8JR_story.html.

on Bunch's childhood: Lonnie Bunch III, "Remembering My Past: The Wisdom of Not Trying to Fight Uphill," *Call the Lost Dream Back: Essays on History, Race and Museums* (Washington, DC: AAM Press, 2010), pp. 18–19, 21.

"a story all Americans . . .": Jacqueline Trescott and J. Freedom Du Lac, "New African American Museum Inspires Celebration, Worries Among Competitors," *Washington Post*, February 18, 2012.

Bunch's Stanford University talk: Lonnie G. Bunch III, "The Challenge of Creating a National Museum," annual Anne and Loren Kieve Distinguished Speaker lecture, Stanford University, May 5, 2011. http://ccsre.stanford.edu/newsletter-art/harriet-tubman-parliament-funkadelic-lonnie-bunch-envisions-national-museum-african-a.

"she's striving . . .": B. Denise Hawkins, "Making the Past Present," *Diverse*, February 9, 2006. http://diverseeducation.com/article/5483/.

"a cruise in uncharted waters . . .": Marisol Bello, "Obama, Laura Bush Break Ground for African American Museum," *USA Today*, February, 22, 2012. http://usatoday30.usatoday.com/news/destinations/story/2012-02-21/New-museum-to-carry-the-weight-of-black-history/53199204/1.

GO TREASURE HUNTING

"While the museum will talk . . .": Kate Taylor, "The Thorny Path to a National Black Museum," *The New York Times*, January 22, 2011.

Bunch's encounter in Austin: "African American Museum Begins to Take Shape," narrated by Guy Raz, *All Things Considered*, NPR, January 9, 2010. http://www.npr.org/templates/story/story.php?storyId=122403151.

BUILD A FITTING HOME

"The choice of design . . .": Philip Kennicott, "One Design Stands Out in African American History and Culture Museum Competition," *Washington Post*, April 7, 2009. http://www.washingtonpost.com/wp-dyn/content/article/2009/04/06/AR2009040603808.html?sid=ST2009040701623.

"Celebration and praise": Smithsonian Institution, "National Museum of African American History & Culture Architect Named," YouTube video, 12:38, April 14, 2009. https://www.youtube.com/watch?v=DkaURDptuIQ&list=PLD6B433185AF1609&index=30.

"Our scheme is quite soaring . . .": Jacqueline Trescott, "Designer Chosen for Black History Museum," *Washington Post*, April 15, 2009. http://www.washingtonpost.com/wp-dyn/content/story/2009/04/07/ST2009040701623.html?sid=ST2009040701623.

"Today, in the words of . . .": Smithsonian Institution, "NMAAHC Groundbreaking Ceremony—Full," YouTube video, 1:23:38, March 12, 2012. https://www.youtube.com/watch?v=aXbKgh2d2uE.

"What we are witnessing . . .": "Rep. John Lewis Speaker at Groundbreaking of National Museum He Helped Establish," John Lewis Official Website, February 22, 2012. http://johnlewis.house.gov/press-release/rep-john-lewis-speaker-groundbreaking-national-museum-he-helped-establish.

"This day has been . . .": Mark Memmott, "'A Long Time Coming,' Obama Says of African-American Museum," *The Two-Way*, NPR, February 22, 2012. http://www.npr.org/sections/thetwo-way/2012/02/22/147260794/a-long-time-coming-obama-says-of-african-american-museum.

"If you think about . . ." Daniel J. Sernovitz, "Behind the Fences of the Smithsonian's African American Museum," *Washington Business Journal*, December 26, 2013, http://www.bizjournals.com/washington/breaking_ground/2013/12/behind-the-fences-of-the-smithsonians.html.

"I built that!": Clark/Smoot/Russell newsletter, Spring 2013.

WELCOME THE WORLD

"Whether your family's . . .": "Assembling Artifacts of African-American History," narrated by Susan Stamberg, *Morning Edition*, NPR, January 14, 2009. http://www.npr.org/templates/story/story.php?storyId=99259871.

"We want to bring everything . . .": Mike Boehm, "Lonnie Bunch Reflects on Journey to National Museum," *Los Angeles Times*, October 28, 2014. http://touch.latimes.com/#section/-1/article/p2p-81799280/.

INDEX

Note: Page numbers in *italics* refer to illustrations.